This Notebook Belongs To

Made in the USA
Las Vegas, NV
14 September 2021

30280002R00069